Easy Windows 11 for seniors 2024

Master easy ways and steps to get the best Windows 11 experience as a senior

Steve Hopkins

Copyright

personal, non-commercial transitory viewing only. This is the grant of a license, not a transfer of title, and under this license you may not:

- modify or copy the work;
- use the work for any commercial purpose, or for any public display (commercial or non-commercial);
- attempt to decompile or reverse engineer any software contained within the work;
- remove any copyright or other proprietary notations from the work; or
- transfer the work to another person or "mirror" the work on any other server.

This license shall automatically terminate if you violate any of these restrictions and may be terminated by Stella Wilson at any time. Upon terminating your viewing of these materials or upon the termination of this license, you must destroy any downloaded materials in your possession whether in electronic or printed format.

For permissions requests, inquiries, or licensing agreements, please contact Stella Wilson

By accessing or using this work you agree to abide by the terms of this copyright notice.

Table of contents

Copyright

Introduction

Chapter One

Chapter two

Personalizing Your Desktop Background

    Adjusting Display Settings for Better Visibility

    Changing Themes and Colors:

    Open Settings:

    Setting Up Accessibility Options:

Chapter Three: Understanding File Explorer

Chapter Four: Installing and Uninstalling Programs

Chapter Five:Browsing the Web with Microsoft Edge: Opening Microsoft Edge

Chapter Six

Chapter Seven

Chapter Eight

Chapter Nine

Chapter Nine

GRATITUDE SPEECH

Dear readers,

Here I am with a grateful heart. It is with immense joy and appreciation that I extend my sincerest thanks to each and every one of you who have purchased my books on Amazon Kindle Direct Publishing (KDP).

Your support and belief in my work mean more to me than words can express. Every time you choose to invest in one of my creations, you not only support my passion but also become an integral part of my journey as an author.

Writing is a solitary endeavor, but your readership transforms it into a shared experience. Your reviews, feedback, and encouragement fuel my creativity and drive me to continue pushing boundaries and exploring new horizons in storytelling.

Each book I publish is a labor of love, crafted with the hope of touching hearts, sparking imaginations, and perhaps even leaving a lasting impact on those who delve into its pages. Knowing that my words have resonated with you in some way fills me with a profound sense of purpose and fulfillment.

I am deeply grateful for your trust and loyalty, for it is your unwavering support that allows me to pursue my dreams and pursue my passion for writing. As I continue on this journey, I carry your kindness and encouragement with me, drawing strength from the knowledge that I am blessed with such an incredible community of readers.

So, from the depth of my heart, thank you. Thank you for choosing my books, thank you for believing in me, and thank you for being a part of this wonderful adventure. I am forever grateful for your support, and I look forward to sharing many more stories with you in the future.

With heartfelt appreciation,

Steve Hopkins

Introduction

Welcome to "Easy Windows 11 for Seniors"! This book is designed to be your comprehensive guide to navigating  the latest iteration of Microsoft's operating system, Windows 11, specifically tailored to meet the needs of seniors. Whether you're a newcomer to the world of computers or looking to upgrade your skills to keep pace with the latest technology trends, this book is here to support you every step of the way.

Technology has become an integral part of our daily lives, offering countless opportunities for communication, entertainment, and productivity. However, for many seniors, the prospect of learning how to use a new operating system can seem daunting and overwhelming. That's where this book comes in – to demystify Windows 11 and make it accessible and easy to understand for users of all experience levels.

In "Easy Windows 11 for Seniors," you'll find clear, step-by-step instructions accompanied by helpful illustrations and screenshots, making it simple to follow along and apply what you learn to your own computer. From basic tasks like navigating the desktop and opening programs to more advanced topics such as customizing settings and staying safe online, each chapter is carefully crafted to empower you with the knowledge and confidence to use Windows 11 effectively.

Throughout the book, we'll focus on providing practical tips and techniques that are specifically tailored to the needs and preferences of seniors. Whether you prefer large fonts for better readability, keyboard shortcuts to minimize mouse usage, or voice commands for hands-free operation, we'll explore a variety of options to help you customize Windows 11 to suit your individual needs.

Additionally, "Easy Windows 11 for Seniors" is more than just a technical manual – it's a resource that emphasizes the importance of enjoying technology and staying connected with loved ones. With Windows 11 as your digital gateway, you'll discover new ways to communicate with family and friends, explore hobbies and interests online, and enrich your life in countless ways.

So, if you're ready to embark on a journey of discovery and empowerment with Windows 11, let's dive in together! Whether you're a complete beginner or an experienced user looking to brush up on your skills, this book is your go-to resource for mastering Windows 11 with ease and confidence. Get ready to unlock the full potential of your computer and embrace the possibilities of the digital age – it's never too late to start your adventure!

Moving from windows 10 to windows 11

With the release of Windows 11, many users are considering making the move from Windows 10 to the latest version of Microsoft's operating system. This change can bring several benefits, including better speed, enhanced security features, and a more modern user experience. In this guide, we'll walk you through the steps to move from Windows 10 to Windows 11, as well as show some of the benefits of Windows 11 over its predecessor.

Step 1: Check Compatibility

Before you begin the update process, it's important to ensure that your device fits the system needs for Windows 11. Microsoft has added some new hardware needs with Windows 11, such as TPM 2.0 (Trusted Platform Module) and Secure Boot support. You can use the PC Health Check tool offered by Microsoft to check if your device is compatible with Windows 11.

Step 2: Backup Your Data

As with any operating system update, it's crucial to back up your important info before continuing. While the update process generally saves your files and settings, there's always a chance of something going wrong. Be sure to back up your papers, photos, videos, and any other important files to an external storage device or cloud service.

Step 3: Download and Install Windows 11

Once you've confirmed compatibility and saved up your info, you can proceed with getting and installing Windows 11. Microsoft offers several ways for switching to Windows 11, including:

Windows Update: If your computer is qualified for the free update to Windows 11, you should receive a notice via Windows Update. You can then follow the on-screen steps to download and install the update.

Media Creation Tool: Alternatively, you can use the Media Creation Tool offered by Microsoft to make installation media for Windows 11. This way allows you to make a clean update of Windows 11 or switch from Windows 10 using the installation disk.

ISO File: If you wish, you can grab the Windows 11 ISO file straight from the Microsoft website and use it to make installation media or run a clean installation.

Follow the steps during the download process, and be sure to pick the choice to keep your files and apps if you're updating from Windows 10.

Step 4: Customize Your Settings
Once the update is complete, you can modify your settings in Windows 11 to fit your tastes. Explore the new features and settings available in Windows 11, such as the updated Start menu, taskbar, and better multitasking capabilities.

Advantages of Windows 11 Over Windows 10:

Redesigned User Interface: Windows 11 features a sleek and modern user interface with rounded edges, new animations, and updated buttons, offering a more finished and visually appealing experience compared to Windows 10.

Improved Performance: Windows 11 is designed for current systems, giving better performance and faster boot times than Windows 10. The new operating system also brings improvements such as DirectStorage, which improves game start times and general system speed.

Enhanced Productivity Features: Windows 11 brings several productivity-focused features, such as Snap Layouts and Snap Groups, which make it easier to organize and work with multiple windows. The new virtual desktops feature also allows users to make separate screens for different jobs or projects.

Better Gaming Experience: For gamers, Windows 11 brings several changes, including support for Auto HDR, which enhances the visual quality of supported games, and DirectStorage, which allows faster loading times and better gaming.

Enhanced Security: Windows 11 includes several security improvements, such as a remade Windows Defender with better malware detection powers, hardware-based security features like TPM 2.0, and enhanced ransomware protection.

Integration with Microsoft Teams: Windows 11 links Microsoft Teams directly into the desktop, making it easy to meet and work with friends, family, and peers through text, voice, and video calls.

Chapter One

Getting Started with Windows 11

Welcome to the exciting world of Windows 11! In this chapter, we'll embark on a journey to explore the foundational elements of Microsoft's latest operating system. Whether you're

brand new to computers or transitioning from an older version of Windows, understanding the basics of Windows 11 is essential for a smooth and enjoyable computing experience.

Navigating the Desktop

Navigating the desktop in Windows 11 is an important skill for seniors to learn, as it gives access to various tools, apps, and files. Here's a full description on how adults can navigate the screen in Windows 11:

Navigating the Desktop in Windows 11 for Seniors

1.   Understanding   the   Desktop Environment: The desktop is the main area in Windows 11, where you'll find icons, links, and tools that provide quick access to important functions and applications. When you first start your computer or log in to Windows 11, you'll see the desktop presented on your screen.

2. Identifying Desktop Icons and Shortcuts: Desktop icons indicate links to files, folders, apps, or system settings. Common screen icons include "This PC" (formerly known as "My Computer"), "Recycle Bin", and links to frequently used apps like Microsoft Edge or File Explorer.

3. Navigating Desktop Icons: To open a program or file indicated by a desktop icon, simply double-click on the icon using the left mouse button. Alternatively, you can use the arrow keys on your computer to travel to the desired button, then press the "Enter" key to open it.

4. Interacting with the Taskbar: The taskbar is a horizontal bar found at the bottom of the screen that gives quick access to frequently used apps, system

icons, and the Start button. You can move the taskbar using the mouse cursor or keyboard tools.

To open a program added to the taskbar, click on its icon with the left mouse button. Use the Windows key on your computer to open the Start menu, then move through the menu using the arrow keys to pick and open apps.

5. Exploring the Start Menu: The Start screen is a primary point for getting apps, settings, files, and more in Windows 11. To open the Start menu, click on the Windows button found in the bottom at the left area of the screen or press the Windows key on your computer. Use the arrow keys on your computer to move through the Start menu choices, including saved apps, newly added apps, and suggested

content. Press the "Enter" key to open a chosen app or item from the Start menu.

6. Using Widgets for Quick Access: Widgets are adjustable mini-applications that provide at-a-glance information and quick access to important features, such as weather reports, news updates, and scheduling events. To view widgets, click on the Widgets button found on the taskbar or press the Windows key + W on your computer. Use the arrow keys to move through the widgets panel and pick the tool you want to work with. Press the "Enter" key to open a chosen window and view more information or interact with its content.

7. Customizing the Desktop: Seniors can personalize their screen to fit their tastes and make it more visually appealing and approachable. Right-click on an empty area of the desktop to access choices for changing the desktop theme, screen size, and display

settings. Choose "Personalize" from the context menu to access settings for changing the screen background, fonts, colors, and more. Use the arrow keys or mouse control to move through the custom settings and make changes as needed. By learning these methods, seniors can easily navigate the desktop in Windows 11, getting important tools and apps with ease and efficiency.

Understanding the basics of Windows 11 is crucial for users of all experience levels. By mastering the foundational elements of the operating system, you'll be better equipped to navigate its features, personalize your desktop, and organize your files effectively. Whether you're using Windows 11 for work, entertainment, or communication, a solid understanding of its core principles will enhance your overall computing experience.

What's Next:

In the following chapters, we'll delve deeper into the various aspects of Windows 11, including customization options, productivity tools, and security features. Get ready to unlock the full potential of your computer and discover new ways to stay connected, productive, and entertained in the digital age.

Chapter two

Personalizing Your Desktop Background

Making changes to your Windows 11 desktop background is a fun way to make your computer feel more like home and add a personal touch. You can use a favorite picture as your background or pick one of the built-in wallpapers in Windows 11.

Step 1: Going to the settings for personalization

To start making your desktop image unique, right-click on an empty spot on your desktop. A choice will show up in the environment. "Personalize" can be found on the page. You can also hit the Start button and then select the gear icon for Settings to get to the custom settings. In the Settings window, choose "Personalization" from the left menu.

Step 2: Pick out a background picture

Once you're in the Personalization settings, click on "Background" from the left menu. Here, you'll see different choices for picking your screen background. You can pick from a collection of pre-installed backgrounds offered by Windows 11, or you can use your own unique picture. To choose a built-in picture, simply click on the image you like, and it will automatically set as your background.

Step 3: Setting Custom Background Image

If you want to use your own photo as the screen background, click on the "Browse" button under the "Choose your picture" area. This will allow you to travel to the place on your computer where your chosen picture is saved. Once you've chosen the image, click "Choose picture" to set it as your screen background.

Step 4: Adjusting Background Settings

Windows 11 also allows you to modify how your background is presented. You can choose to fit the picture to your screen, stretch it, tile it, or fill the screen while keeping the aspect ratio. Additionally, you can pick multiple photos to make a movie, with choices to change the picture at defined times.

Step 5: Applying the Changes

Once you've chosen your preferred background picture and changed the settings to your liking, simply close the Personalization settings window. Your changes will be made immediately, and you'll see your new desktop background presented on your screen.

Additional Tips for Seniors:

If you're having trouble finding the right picture for your background, try asking a family member or friend to help you pick one. Experiment with different background pictures and settings until you find the combo that suits you best.
Don't be afraid to change your desktop background regularly to keep your computer experience new and fun.

Adjusting Display Settings for Better Visibility

Adjusting display settings in Windows 11 to increase sight, especially for seniors, can greatly improve their computer experience. Here lies a step-by-step guide to changing these settings:

Accessing Display Settings:
Click on the Start button (Windows sign) found at the bottom left corner of the screen.
Select the Settings button (gear-shaped) from the Start menu to open the Settings app.

Navigate to Display Settings:
In the Settings app, click on the "System" choice.
On the left column, select "Display."
Adjusting Text Size:

Under the "Scale and layout" part, you'll find a tool called "Change the size of text, apps, and other items."
Increase the scale to make writing and other features bigger. This will make everything on the computer easy to read.

Adjusting Resolution:
Below the text size control, you'll see the "Display resolution" part.
Click on the dropdown menu to pick a smaller size if the current one makes parts too small. Lower sizes may make parts appear bigger but might reduce the clarity of pictures and text.

High Contrast Mode:
Scroll down in the Display settings to find the "High contrast mode" part.
Toggle on "High contrast mode" to allow it. This mode changes colors to improve contrast, making writing and pictures easier to distinguish for those with eye problems.

Cursor and Pointer Settings:
In the Display settings, click on "Advanced display settings" found under the "Multiple displays" area. Here, you can change mouse and pointer size. Increase the scale to make the pointer bigger and more noticeable.

Night Light:
Night Light lowers blue light output, which can help reduce eye pain, especially when using the computer at night. In the Display options, click on "Night light" in the left tab. Toggle on "Night light" to allow it and change the strength and time according to taste.

Customize Contrast and Brightness:
Some monitors offer built-in settings to change color and brightness. Seniors may prefer stronger contrast to make words and pictures stand out more.

If your monitor has actual buttons for changes, use them to improve contrast and brightness.

Magnifier Tool:
Windows also offers a built-in Magnifier tool to zoom in on parts of the screen. Press the Windows key and the plus (+) key simultaneously to open Magnifier. Use the plus and minus keys to change the zoom level.

Accessibility Features:
Windows 11 gives various accessibility tools, such as Narrator (screen reader), Speech recognition, and Eye control, which can further help adults with visual problems.

Changing Themes and Colors:

Open Settings: Click on the Windows button in the bottom left part of the screen.

Select the gear button titled "Settings" to open the Settings app.

Access Personalization Settings:
In the Settings app, select the "Personalization" area.

Choose a Theme:
Under the "Personalization" choices, click on "Themes" on the left menu.
You'll see a list of possible themes. Click on a theme to explore it.

Customize Colors:
Navigate to the "Colors" tab in the Personalization settings. Here, you can choose between light and dark mode and adjust accent colors. You can also select "Automatically pick an accent

color from my background" for a changing accent color.

Adjust Advanced Settings (Optional):
For more customization choices, try the "Backgrounds," "Lock screen," and "Start" tabs under Personalization.

Setting Up Accessibility Options:

Open Settings:
Follow the steps described earlier to open the Settings app.

Access Accessibility Settings:
In the Settings app, pick the "Accessibility" area.

Explore Available Options:
Windows 11 gives different disability tools such as Magnifier, High Contrast, Narrator, Speech Recognition, etc.

Click on each option to learn more and adjust settings as needed.

For example, to activate the Magnifier, click on "Magnifier" and change the switch to "On." Adjust the settings according to tastes.

Use Ease of Access Keyboard Shortcuts:
Press Windows logo key + Ctrl + '+' to zoom in and Windows logo key + Ctrl + '-' to zoom out.

Managing Files and Folders:
Open File Explorer:
Click on the folder icon in the taskbar or press Windows logo key + E to open File Explorer.

Navigate Folders:
Use the toolbar on the left to move to different files such as Documents, Downloads, Pictures, etc.

Organize Files:

To make a new folder, right-click in the chosen spot, select "New," and then "Folder." Name the area properly. To move things, click and drag them to the desired place. To delete files, pick the file(s) and press the Delete key.

Search for Files:
Use the search bar in the top right part of File Explorer to quickly find files and folders.

Adjust View Settings:
Click on the "View" tab in File Explorer to change settings such as icon size, sorting choices, and preview bar display.

Backup Important Files:
Consider setting up regular saves using Windows Backup or utilizing cloud storage services like OneDrive for added security.

Chapter Three:
Understanding File Explorer

File Explorer is an important tool in Windows 11 that allows users to organize, control, and access files and folders on their computer. For adults, who might be new to computers or need a simpler description, knowing how to use File Explorer can greatly improve their working experience. Here's a full guide designed for seniors:

Navigating File Explorer:
Open File Explorer by clicking on its button in the taskbar or by pressing Win + E keys. The left pane shows quick access files like Desktop, Downloads, Documents, Pictures, etc. You can click on any of these to quickly travel to those places.

The main window shows the items of the chosen folder. You can scroll through the files and folders to find what you need.

Organizing Files and Folders:
To make a new folder, right-click in the main window, select "New," and then "Folder." Give your folder a name and press Enter. To move files or folders, simply drag and drop them from one place to another. You can also use cut (Ctrl + X) and paste (Ctrl + V) tools.
To rename a file or folder, right-click on it, select "Rename," type the new name, and press Enter.

Deleting Files and Folders:
To delete a file or folder, right-click on it and pick "Delete." Alternatively, you can press the Delete key after choosing the file or folder. Windows will ask for permission before completely deleting the thing. Click "Yes" to confirm.

Using Search to Find Files Quickly:

File Explorer has a strong search tool to help you find things quickly. Simply click on the search box in the top right corner and type the name of the file you're looking for. As you type, File Explorer will start showing similar files and folders. You can click on the appropriate result to open it.

Working with Applications:

You can easily reach loaded apps through File Explorer. Navigate to "This PC" in the left pane and then open the "Local Disk (C:)" or whichever drive you have your apps loaded on. Look for the "Program Files" or "Program Files (x86)" folder. This is where most apps are stored. Double-click on the folder matching to the program you want to use, then find and double-click on the application's main file (usually finishing with .exe) to start it.

Chapter Four: Installing and Uninstalling Programs

Installing Programs:
Download the installation file for the chosen program from a trusted source or place the installation CD/DVD into your machine. Double-click the installation file. This will usually have a .exe ending. Follow the on-screen directions in the installation process. Typically, you'll need to agree to the terms and conditions, choose the download spot, and select any extra choices. Once the application is complete, you may find the program's link on the desktop or in the Start Menu.

Uninstalling Programs:
Open Settings by tapping on the Start button and choosing the gear icon, or by pressing Win + I.

Click on "Apps" in the Settings menu.
Scroll through the list of loaded apps and find the one you want to remove.
Click on the app, then click on the "Uninstall" button that shows.
Follow the on-screen directions to finish the removal process.

Launching Applications from the Start Menu:

Using the Start Menu: Click on the Start button found at the bottom left corner of the screen, or press the Windows key on your computer. The Start Menu will show, presenting a list of commonly used and recently added apps. Scroll through the list to find the program you want to start, then click on it to open.

Managing Open Windows and Applications:

Switching Between Applications:
To switch between open apps, you can use the Alt + Tab computer trick. Hold down the Alt key and press the Tab key

frequently to move through open windows. Alternatively, you can use the Task View button found on the desktop to see all open windows and switch between them.

Closing Applications:

To close an application, click on the "X" button found at the top right part of the application window. Alternatively, you can use the Alt + F4 keyboard shortcut.

Creating Shortcuts for Quick Access:

Creating Desktop Shortcuts: Right-click on the application's button in the Start Menu. Select "More" and then "Open file location." Right-click on the application's link in the File Explorer window that opens. Select "Send to" and then "Desktop (create shortcut)."

Internet and Email Basics:

Browsing the Internet:

Open your favorite online browser by clicking on its button in the desktop or Start Menu. Type the website address (URL) into the address bar at the top of the computer window and press Enter. Use the mouse or tablet to click on links and browse through web pages.

Email Basics:
Open your email program (such as Mail or Outlook) by clicking on its button in the taskbar or Start Menu. Sign in to your email account, do this using your email

address and password. To write a new email, click on the "Compose" or "New Email" button and enter the recipient's email address, title, and message. Click on the "Send" button to send the email. These steps provide a thorough guide for adults on downloading and removing programs, starting applications, controlling open windows, making favorites, and using basic internet and email functions in Windows 11. Practicing these tasks daily will help seniors become more comfortable and proficient in using their computers for various reasons.

Chapter Five:Browsing the Web with Microsoft Edge: Opening Microsoft Edge

---

Click on the Microsoft Edge button on your screen or in the menu to start the browser.

Navigating to Websites:

Type the URL of the website you want to visit in the address bar at the top and press Enter. You can also use a search engine like Bing or Google by typing your query directly into the address bar and pressing Enter.

Tabs and Multiple Windows:
To open a new tab, click on the "+" button next to the existing tab or press Ctrl + T. To open a link in a new tab, right-click on the link and select "Open link in new tab." To switch between tabs, click on the tab you want to view.

Bookmarking Favorite Sites:
Click on the star icon in the address bar to bookmark a page. To access your favorites, click on the three dots in the top-right corner, then select "Favorites" and choose the saved site you want to visit.

Customizing Settings:

Click on the three dots in the top-right corner and select "Settings" to adjust your browser experience. Here, you can change different settings like preferred search engine, privacy, and look.

Searching the Internet Effectively:

Using Search Engines:
Type your question into the search engine's search bar and press Enter.
Use specific terms to narrow your search and get more appropriate results.

Filtering Results:
After making a search, use options like date, type, or place to narrow down the results and find what you're looking for more quickly.

Evaluating Sources:
Be cautious of misinformation. Always check the credibility of the website before trusting the information.

Stick to reputable sources such as government websites, academic institutions, or well-known news outlets.

Sending and Receiving Emails with the Mail App:
Opening the Mail App:
Click on the Mail app icon on your desktop or in the taskbar to open the app.

Setting Up an Email Account:
If you haven't already set up an email account, click on "Add Account" and follow the prompts to add your email address and password.

Composing an Email:
Click on "New mail" to compose a new email. Enter the recipient's email address, subject, and body of the email. Click on "Send" when you're ready to send the email.

Reading and Replying to Emails:

Click on an email to read its contents.
To reply, click on "Reply" or "Reply all" if you want to reply to all recipients.

Managing Emails:
Use folders to organize your emails. You can create folders for different categories like "Personal," "Work," or "Shopping." Archive or delete emails you no longer need to keep your inbox clutter-free. Staying Safe Online: Tips and Best Practices:

Keep Software Updated:
Ensure that your Windows 11 operating system, websites, and security tools are up to date to protect against flaws.

Use Strong Passwords:
Create unique and complicated passwords for your online accounts and consider using a password manager to store them safely.

Beware of Phishing Attempts:

Be careful of emails or texts from unknown senders asking for personal information or pushing urgent action. These could be scam efforts trying to steal your information.

Enable Two-Factor Authentication (2FA):
Whenever possible, allow 2FA for your web accounts to add an extra layer of security.

Use Secure Connections:
Look for the padlock sign and "https://" in the address bar when viewing websites to ensure you're using a safe link.

Staying Connected with Contacts:
Using Email:
Use the Mail app to stay in touch with friends and family by sharing and getting letters.

Social Media:

Consider joining social media sites like Facebook or Twitter to meet with friends, family, and groups of interest.

Video Calling:

Use video chatting apps like Skype or Zoom to have face-to-face talks with loved ones, especially if they're far away.

Online Groups and Communities:
Join online groups or clubs connected to your interests or hobbies to meet with like-minded people.

Regular Communication:
Make it a habit to regularly check in with your friends through email, phone calls, or video chats to keep strong relationships.

Chapter Six

Adding and Managing Contacts:

Open the People App: Click on the Start button (Windows icon) on the taskbar, then select "People" from the app list.

Add a New Contact: In the People app, click on the "+" button to add a new contact. Fill in the information such as name, email, phone number, etc.

Change Existing Contacts: To change an existing contact, click on the contact's name, then select the "Edit" choice. Make changes as needed and save.

Making Video Calls with Skype:

Install Skype: If Skype isn't already loaded, you can download it from the Microsoft Store. Open the Store app, look for Skype, and click "Install".

Sign in: Open Skype, and sign in with your Microsoft account. If you don't have one, you can make it.

Find a Contact: Click on the "Contacts" tab, then select the person you want to call. Start a Video Call: Click on the video camera button to start a video call with the chosen friend.

Sending Instant Messages with Microsoft Teams:

Install Microsoft Teams: If Microsoft Teams isn't already loaded, you can download it from the Microsoft Store.

Sign in: Open Teams and sign in with your Microsoft account.

Find a Contact: Click on the "Chat" tab, then select the person you want to write.

Send a Message: Type your message in the chat box at the bottom and press Enter to send.

Syncing Contacts Across Devices:

Using Microsoft Account: Ensure you're signed in to the same Microsoft account on all your devices (PC, smartphone, tablet). Contacts added or changed on one device should instantly sync to others.

Check Sync Settings: Go to Settings > Accounts > Your Info, and ensure that "Sync settings" is turned on. This means contacts are shared across devices.

Managing Photos and Videos:
Open Photos App: Click on the Start button, then select "Photos" from the app list.

Import Photos and Videos: To import photos and videos from your camera or phone, connect the device to your PC. The Photos app should immediately identify and ask you to import.

Order pictures: Use the Albums tool to order your pictures into groups. Click on the "Albums" tab and select "Create new album" to start arranging.

Edit Photos and Videos: Click on a photo or video to watch it, then click on the "Edit & Create" button to access editing tools such as crop, rotate, improve, etc.

Share Photos and Videos: Select the photo or video you want to share, then click on the "Share" button at the top. Choose how you want to share it (email, social media, etc.).

Chapter Seven

Within this chapter lies step by step guide on how to View and Organize Your Photos, edit and Enhance Images with Photos App, watch Videos with Movies & TV App, Transfer photos and videos from Devices specifically and carefully crafted for you my valued reader.

Using Windows 11 for picture and video management, editing, and fun can be a smooth experience, even for adults who may not be as comfortable with technology. Here's a full guide on how to view and organize pictures, edit and improve images, watch videos, move media from devices, and explore entertainment options using Windows 11, designed with seniors in mind:

Viewing and Organizing Photos: Opening Photos App: Start by finding the Photos app in your Start Menu or by looking for it using the search bar. Click on the app to open it.

Viewing pictures: Once the app is open, you'll see all your pictures sorted by date. You can scroll through them to find the one you want to read.

Organizing pictures: To organize your pictures, you can make folders. Click on the three dots (...) in the top right area and select "Albums." Then click on "New album" and give it a name. You can then add pictures to the book by picking them and choosing "Add to" > the name of your album.

Editing and Enhancing Images:

Editing Photos: Open the picture you want to change and click on the "Edit & Create" button at the top. Here you can crop, move, change color and contrast, and add effects to improve your picture.

Enhancing Images: For more detailed editing, you can use the "Adjust" choice to fine-tune settings like brightness, color, and clarity. Experiment with these tools to improve your pictures.

Watching Videos: Opening Movies & TV App: Locate the Movies & TV app in your Start Menu or search for it using the search bar. Click on the app to open it.

Watching Videos: Once the app is open, you can look through your video library or purchase/rent new movies and TV shows from the Microsoft Store. Simply click on the movie you want to watch and hit the play button.

Transferring Photos and Videos from Devices:

Connecting Devices: To move pictures and movies from your camera or smartphone, connect the device to your computer using a USB wire or through Bluetooth.

Importing Media: Windows 11 should immediately recognize your device and ask you to import pictures and movies. Follow the on-screen directions to finish the import process.

Exploring Entertainment Options:

Microsoft Store: Explore the Microsoft Store to find a range of entertainment choices including movies, TV shows, music, and games. You can look through different groups or use the search bar to find specific material.

Streaming Services: Windows 11 allows famous streaming services like Netflix, Hulu, and Disney+. Download the various apps from the Microsoft Store and log in to view your favorite shows and movies.

Xbox Game Pass: If you're interested in games, try subscribing to Xbox Game Pass. This service gives a selection of over 100 high-quality games that you can download and play on your PC.

Tips for Seniors:
Accessibility Features: Take advantage of Windows 11's disability tools such as magnifier, announcer, and high contrast mode to make browsing easy.

One-on-One Training: If you're still unsure about using Windows 11, try getting one-on-one training from a family member, friend, or neighborhood community center.

Take it Slow: Don't feel pushed to learn everything at once. Take your time to discover and play with different aspects at your own pace.

Chapter Eight

In this chapter, let's take a look at the following. Venturing into the following and navigating hitch free will make your experience using Windows 11 a remarkable one.

- Listening to Music with Groove Music
- Watching Movies and TV Shows
- Playing Games with Xbox Game Pass
- Discovering New Content with Microsoft Store
- Keeping Your System Secure

Groove Music is Microsoft's music player and streaming service. Here's how to use it:

Opening Groove Music: Click on the Start button in the lower-left corner of the screen, type "Groove Music", and click on the Groove Music app when it shows.

Finding Music: You can listen to music you've bought, or explore new music through Groove Music's streaming service.

Playing Music: Once you've found a song or album you want to listen to, simply click on it to start playing.

Creating Playlists: You can make playlists of your best songs by clicking on the "New Playlist" button and adding songs to it.

Adjusting choices: Groove Music has choices to change playing quality, equalization settings, and more. Click on the gear button in the bottom-left corner to open settings.

Watching Movies and TV Shows:

Using Microsoft Movies & TV: This is Microsoft's built-in app for watching movies and TV shows.

Finding Content: Open the app by tapping on the Start button, typing "Movies & TV", and clicking on the app. You can buy or rent movies and TV shows from the Microsoft Store.

Playing Content: Once you've bought or rented a movie or TV show, it will appear in your library. Click on it to start watching.

Adjusting Settings: You can change settings such as subtitles and playing quality within the app.

Playing Games with Xbox Game Pass:

Subscribing to Xbox Game Pass: Xbox Game Pass is a monthly service that gives you access to a selection of games. You can join by visiting the Xbox website.

Installing Games: Once you're registered, you can download and install games from the Xbox app on Windows 11. Click on the Start button, type "Xbox", and click on the Xbox app to open it. Then, head to the Game Pass area to view and install games.

Playing Games: After downloading a game, you can launch it from the Xbox app and start playing. The app also offers features like awards and friends groups.

Discovering New Content with Microsoft Store:

Browsing the Microsoft Store: The Microsoft Store is where you can find apps, games, movies, TV shows, and more.

Finding Content: Open the Microsoft Store by tapping on the Start button, typing "Microsoft Store", and clicking on the app. You can browse different topics or use the search bar to find specific material.

Installing Content: Once you've found something you want, click on it to read more information and then click the "Install" button to download and install it.

Keeping the System Secure:

Windows changes: Windows regularly makes changes to improve security and efficiency. Make sure to keep your system up-to-date by letting Windows to run updates automatically.

Antivirus Software: Consider running antivirus software to protect your system from malware and viruses. Windows Defender is built into Windows and offers basic protection, but you may also want to explore third-party antivirus software for additional features.

Safe Browsing Practices: Be careful when viewing the internet and avoid clicking on strange links or getting files from unknown sources. Use safe passwords for your accounts and consider using a password manager to keep track of them.

Firewall: Windows includes a built-in firewall that helps prevent unwanted entry to your computer. Make sure it's turned on by going to Settings > Update & Security > Windows Security > Firewall & network security.

Backup Your Data: Regularly backup your important files and papers to an extra hard drive or cloud storage service to protect them from loss or damage.

Chapter Nine

These are the topics to be explored for easy digestion in this chapter.

- Understanding Windows Security Features
- Installing Updates and Patches
- Using Antivirus Software for Added Protection
- Practicing Safe Browsing Habits
- Troubleshooting Common Issues

Understanding Windows Security Features:

Windows Defender: Antivirus and Antimalware *Protection:* Windows Defender, now called Microsoft Defender Antivirus, works quietly in the background to protect your computer from viruses, malware, and other risks. It checks files and websites in real-time to identify and remove any harmful material.

How to Access It: Windows Security, where Windows Defender lives, can be reached by tapping on the Start button, typing "Windows Security," and choosing the app. From there, you can see the present state of their device's protection, run scans, and change settings if needed.

User Account Control (UAC): Permission Control: User Account Control (UAC) asks you for permission whenever a job needs management powers, such as downloading software or making system changes. This stops unwanted changes to your machine.

How to Interact With It: As a senior, you will see UAC prompts when trying to load new software or make system changes. Ensure to read the prompts carefully before continuing and ensure they trust the source of the action.

Secure Boot: Boot Process Security: Secure Boot protects your computer during the boot process by only allowing known apps to load. This helps avoid malware attempts that target the boot process.

How you can Understand It: As a senior , you may not deal directly with Secure Boot settings, but they can be comforted that Windows 11 includes this tool to keep their system secure.

Installing Updates and Patches:

Automatic Updates:

Set Automatic Updates: You can set automatic updates by going to Settings > Windows Update > Advanced choices, and ensuring the "Automatic" option is chosen under "Choose when updates are installed."

How to Manage It: Once automatic updates are set, you don't need to worry about physically loading patches. Windows will download and install them in the background, keeping their system safe and up-to-date.

Manual Updates: Check for Updates: As a Senior, you can directly check for updates by going to Settings > Windows Update and clicking on "Check for updates."

How to Do It: If you prefer to directly check for changes, you can follow these steps regularly to ensure your system is up-to-date. You should run any important changes quickly to keep security.

Using Antivirus Software for Added Protection:

Third-Party Antivirus Software:

Install Reputable Software: You can install third-party security software from reputable companies to add an extra layer of safety to their machine.

How to Choose It: Choose well-known protection software with good reviews and scores by asking for suggestions from friends, family, or trusted computer help experts.

Real-Time Scanning: Real-Time Protection: Antivirus software offers real-time scanning, which continuously watches files and web activity for signs of malware.

How to Can Utilize It: Once loaded, ensure that real-time checking is allowed in their security program options. This offers ongoing defense against threats without needing regular scans.

Practicing Safe Browsing Habits:

Web Browser Security: Keep Browsers Updated: Ensure that the web browser is up-to-date to benefit from the latest security fixes and features.

How to Maintain It: Set your browser to update automatically or directly check for changes by visiting the browser's settings menu.

Password Security: Strong Passwords: Use strong, unique passwords for your accounts and consider using a password manager to help them remember their passwords safely.

How to Implement It: Password organizers like LastPass or Bitwarden can create and store complicated passwords for seniors, lowering the load of memory.

Troubleshooting Common Issues:

Performance Issues:

Check Resource Usage: As a senior, you can use Task Manager to check if any apps are using a large amount of system resources, possibly causing speed problems.

How to Access It: Task Manager can be opened by hitting Ctrl + Shift + Esc or by right-clicking on the desktop and choosing "Task Manager."

Software Compatibility:

Compatibility Mode: If you find compatibility problems with older software, you can try starting it in compatibility mode by right-clicking on the program's executable file, choosing "Properties," and going to the "Compatibility" option.

How to Try It: If a program isn't working correctly, you can right-click on its folder or executable file, select "Properties," and follow the steps to run it in compatibility mode.

Internet Connectivity Problems:

Restart Router/Modem: Seniors can fix internet connection issues by restarting their router or modem, which can often address temporary network problems.

How to Do It: You can unplug your router or modem from the power source, wait for a few seconds, and then plug it back in. Be patient enough for the devices to restart and try rejoining the internet.

Chapter Nine

Within this chapter lies a detailed view of the following which is crafted to aid you in your experience with your windows 11 as a senior.

- Identifying and Resolving Software Errors
- Fixing Internet Connection Problems
- Troubleshooting Hardware Issues
- Getting Help from Microsoft Support

Now, let's take them one after another.

Identifying and Resolving Software Errors:

Identify the mistake Message: When facing a software mistake, note down any error messages visible on the screen. These messages often provide useful information about the source of the problem.

Restart the Computer: Many program problems can be fixed simply by restarting the computer. Click on the Start button, then the Power icon, and choose "Restart."

Check for Updates: Ensure that Windows 11 and all your loaded apps are up-to-date. Go to Settings > Windows Update, and click on "Check for updates." Install any available patches.

Run System File Checker (SFC): SFC is a built-in tool in Windows that checks and fixes damaged system files. Open Command Prompt as an administrator (look for "cmd" in the Start menu, right-click on Command Prompt, and pick "Run as administrator"). Then type sfc /scannow and press Enter.

Perform a System Restore: If the problem started recently, you can use System Restore to return your computer to a previous working state. Search for

"System Restore" in the Start menu and follow the on-screen directions.

Fixing Internet and Connection Problems:

Check Physical Connections: Ensure all cords (Ethernet, power, etc.) are safely linked to your machine and router/modem.

Restart Modem/Router: Unplug the power cord from your modem/router, wait for about 30 seconds, and then plug it back in. Wait a few minutes for the device to restart.

Check Network Settings: Go to Settings > Network & Internet. Check if Wi-Fi is turned on and if your network is listed. You can also fix network bugs from this page.

Update Network Drivers: Outdated network drivers can cause connection issues. Right-click on the Start button, select Device Manager, expand the Network devices group, right-click on your network adapter, and select "Update driver."

Troubleshooting Hardware Issues:
Check Device Connections: Ensure that all devices (keyboard, mouse, printer, etc.) are properly linked to your machine.

Run Hardware Diagnostics: Windows 11 has built-in diagnostic tools that can help spot hardware problems. Search for "Windows Memory Diagnostic" in the Start menu to check your computer's memory, or search for "Troubleshoot" and pick "Hardware and Devices" to run the hardware troubleshooter.

Check for Overheating: Overheating can cause hardware problems. Make sure your computer's vents are not blocked, and consider using a laptop cooling pad if necessary.

Getting Help from Microsoft Support:
Microsoft Support Website: Visit the Microsoft Support website (support.microsoft.com) for self-help tools, including debugging tips and knowledge base pieces.

Contact Microsoft Support: If you're unable to fix the problem on your own, you can contact Microsoft Support directly for help. Visit support.microsoft.com/contactus to find the proper contact way based on your area and problem.

Community boards: Microsoft also runs community boards where users can ask questions and seek help from other users and Microsoft MVPs.

Virtual Support: Microsoft may offer virtual support choices such as chat or online assistance, where a support person can help identify and fix the problem directly.

Conclusion

As we reach the end of "Easy Windows 11 for Seniors 2024," it's clear that age is no barrier to mastering the latest technology. Throughout this journey, we've explored the ins and outs of Microsoft's newest operating system, Windows 11, tailored specifically for the needs and preferences of seniors. From navigating the desktop to customizing settings, communicating online, and staying safe in the digital world, this book has served as your trusted guide every step of the way. In today's fast-paced and ever-evolving digital landscape, it's essential for seniors to feel confident and empowered in using technology to enrich their lives. With Windows 11 as your digital companion, you've gained the skills and knowledge to stay connected with loved ones, explore new hobbies and interests, and unleash your creativity like never before. But our journey doesn't end here. As technology continues to evolve, so too will your skills and confidence in using it. Remember, learning is a lifelong journey, and every challenge you overcome opens the door to new opportunities and experiences. So, as you embark on your next digital adventure, whether it's mastering a new app, exploring social media, or diving deeper into the world of Windows 11, know that you have the tools and resources at your fingertips to succeed. Embrace the digital age with enthusiasm and curiosity, and never hesitate to seek help or guidance when needed. Thank you for joining us on this journey through "Easy Windows 11 for Seniors 2024." May your future in the digital world be filled with endless possibilities, creativity, and joy. Happy computing!

Warm regards,

Steve Hopkins

Index

- Introduction to Windows 11
- Getting Started with Your Computer
- Turning On and Logging In
- Exploring the Desktop
- Understanding the Start Menu
- Navigating Windows 11

- Using File Explorer
- Customizing the Taskbar
- Mastering Keyboard Shortcuts
- Working with Applications
- Using Microsoft Edge for Browsing
- Managing Emails with Mail
- Exploring Office Apps: Word, Excel, PowerPoint
- Customizing Your Experience
- Personalizing Your Desktop Background
- Adjusting Display Settings
- Setting Up Accessibility Features
- Staying Secure Online
- Understanding Internet Safety
- Configuring Firewall and Antivirus
- Recognizing Online Scams
- Connecting with Others
- Using Skype for Video Calls
- Exploring Social Media Integration
- Sharing Files and Folders
- Troubleshooting Common Issues
- Fixing Slow Performance
- Resolving Software Errors
- Getting Help from Support

- Advanced Features for Power Users
- Virtual Desktops and Task View
- Using Windows Defender for Enhanced Security
- Exploring Cloud Storage with OneDrive
- Conclusion and Further Resources